Praise for *Ignite*

"If you want to learn an extremely effective method for dreaming BIG that will also help you to make your dreams come true, Ignite is the book to get you there. Explained with a combination of simplicity, entertainment and profound wisdom from Mitch – with beautiful visual authorship by Jocelyn – this is a book you can enjoy and benefit from either by yourself, or together with the person with whom you are building your magnificent dream. It's also a great book to get for that young person you know who has a dream inside them, but needs just a bit of help communicating it…to themselves."

Bob Burg
Co-author of National Best Seller, 'The Go-Giver'
CEO, Burg Communications
www.Burg.com

"When it comes to going after BIG dreams, Mitch helps people get out of their own way. His wise counsel is a blend of pragmatic suggestions and inspirational stories that will get you thinking AND doing. Whether you know exactly what your dream is or you don't have a clue — Mitch will help you discover just how to make it happen!"

Drew McLellan
Author, Speaker and Blogger
Top Dog, McLellan Marketing
DrewsMarketingMinute.com

"The questions posed in Ignite will be just the spark you need to get moving on a dream you previously put on hold (or didn't even know you had!). This book is a winner! Mitch is my go-to guy when it comes to dreaming BIG! The bottom line is he helps people get done what seems impossible by asking questions that you'd never ask yourself."

Adam Carroll
Author of the Best Seller, 'Winning The Money Game'
CEO, National Financial Educators

Praise for *Ignite*

"With an encouraging voice, Ignite! delivers a BIG message. This isn't a book, it's a breathtaking experience. The images will capture you, the author's authenticity will move you, and the stories will inspire you. This is not a one-size-fits-all exercise. It is customized to find and fit your BIG dream. Having personally experienced this process, I guarantee you'll never be the same."

Dondi Scumachi
Author of 'Designed for Success,' 'Ready, Set...Grow,' and 'Career Moves'

"You know that BIG dream you have that seems unrealistic and unobtainable? It's not. Everyone has dreams. But few people ever light the spark to make those dreams a reality. Reading this book will do just that."

John Morgan
Author of the best seller, 'Brand Against the Machine'

"This wonderful little book will be a modern day treasure map to help you excavate those buried dreams and spark your passions again!"

Patricia Rossi
NBC Daytime's Etiquette Expert

"Prior to reading the book, I had an inhibition about my potential dream. After reading the book, I realized "I can do it!" Thanks Mitch and Jocelyn for a wonderful book."

Cheri Maben Crouch, Ph.D.

Contents

Contents

3 SIMPLE STEPS FOR
RE-SPARKING
YOUR BURIED DREAMS
AND BUILDING A PLAN THAT
FINALLY WORKS

by MITCH MATTHEWS

**WITH VISUAL AUTHOR
JOCELYN WALLACE**

IGNITE

3 simple steps for re-sparking your buried dreams and building a plan that finally works

**FOR THE ONE
WHO GIVES US
DREAMS.**

FOR I KNOW THE PLANS I HAVE FOR YOU....

How to Use *Ignite*

from Visual Author,
Jocelyn Wallace

When I sat down to work with Mitch on this book, we first wanted to create a clear picture of you, the reader. We got specific about who would read Ignite, how it would be read, when, and where.

You have BIG dreams, but you often keep them to yourself. You drink too much coffee, have more good days than bad, but feel like you are missing something.

Always in a hurry and overloaded with a busy schedule, you don't take time for yourself to think or dream about what could be. And even if you did, you don't know where to start.

Once I could see you clearly, I was determined to uncover the DNA of Mitch's thinking, his mission, and his dream for you.

What he shared with me was remarkable, yet simple. So much so, I made it my mission too.

A fire ignited within me to shoot photos for this book in a creative, playful, yet thought-provoking way. As you read the book, I hope the images encourage you and challenge you. If at first you aren't sure how the photo relates to the story or question, keep looking. The answer is there — within the story, within the image, and within you.

Mitch is the real deal. He is transparent, positive and encouraging. Take your time reading the stories he wrote, and find yourself within them. You won't be disappointed.

This book is organized into three easy sections to help you:

1) **start** dreaming!

2) **act** on your dream! ...and

3) **sustain** your dream!

Following each story, Mitch lined up a series of questions along with some space for you to answer them within this book. Don't skip this step! It's a critical part of igniting your BIG dream into action.

Because of the way Ignite was created, you can experience it while in between all of the places you need to be: waiting in the car, on a bus, train or plane. And no, I am not about to quote my favorite Dr. Seuss book, Green Eggs and Ham.

But I will say with a smile that dreaming BIG has a lot in common with that tale. You might want to resist it at first, but you won't be sorry you tried it! Have fun, enjoy.

Introduction

I grew up in a small town in Iowa.

It was one of those communities with a downtown square filled with small businesses that surrounded the county courthouse. There were a couple of big companies in town and a number of small ones.

You knew everyone in your neighborhood and you even liked most of them!

It was a town where, as a kid, you could ride your bike everywhere and I did just that.

In fact, when I was twelve, I rode my light blue ten-speed to the local bike shop every day of the summer. The shop was right off the square and it was located in a hole-in-the-wall building next to the local Salvation Army.

It was old and it smelled like WD40, but for me it was paradise. I spent hours there. I'd study the shiny new bikes. I'd talk to the owner and the mechanics. I'd pour over the catalogs and learn about the newest trends and products. I just loved it.

I spent so much time there that the following summer the owner and his wife had to decide between having me arrested for loitering or hiring me. I'm wildly grateful to say that they hired me.

And that's how one of my first BIG dreams was realized.

So, at thirteen, I was convinced that this was how it worked. You do the things that you love to do, do them well (or at least often) and you'll get to walk into more and more of your dreams.

It was a simple truth and it had completely worked for me as a 13-year-old.

But… since that time I've figured out that it isn't always that easy. Is it?

Things happen.

Stuff gets tough sometimes.

Businesses leave town. Jobs get lost. People that you love can get sick.

Breakthroughs don't always happen when you hope they will. Sometimes people say "no" when you really need them to say "yes."

And sometimes you celebrate a 9th anniversary at a job that you only hoped to be in for a year.

It can get hard, can't it?

I know. I've been there.

In fact, as you'll find out later in the book, the biggest reason why we started our BIG Dream Gatherings was because I was tired, scared and about ready to give up on our dream.

At that point, I was so worn out that I couldn't even remember what the BIG dream was anymore.

Maybe that's where you're at.

If it is… that's okay.

You're in the right place and you're reading the right book.

Why?

Well, this is a starting place.

Whether you're wildly clear on what some of your BIG dreams are... or you're in a place where you can't even remember the last time you could remember your dreams… It's okay.

We're in this together.

Let's simply agree that it may be harder to go after our goals than I thought it was at 13… but let's also agree that a little child-like enthusiasm can't hurt either.

Right?

So let's do it.

Let's move forward together… with a good mix of cautious optimism and youthful wonder.

Let's just take it one page at a time. And together… we'll ignite your mind and heart.

More importantly… we'll spark your BIG Dreams into action!

Why Dream BIG?

Let's face it. It's been tough for a lot of us lately. And that can make it hard to think about our goals and dreams, let alone begin to go after them.

With my line of work, I get to travel around the country and talk with people about their dreams and goals. And it doesn't matter how old you are, it's simply a tougher time to be dreaming BIG.

Whether you're the college student wanting to make an impact on the world but you're also worrying about the job market when you graduate. Or you're the budding entrepreneur with a revolutionary idea but you're facing a tight schedule and an even tighter budget. Or maybe you're the teacher with a dream to help kids in Africa, but you're strapped to take care of your own students let alone children on the other side of the planet.

There is no doubt. Dreaming BIG... especially now... can be hard.

At the same time, I don't know if there has ever been a more important time for us to be dreaming BIG. Don't you agree?

BIG dreams are what our country has been built on. BIG dreams are what change things for the better. BIG dreams give life flavor, dimension and purpose. You know this. In fact, I'm betting it's the reason why you are reading this now.

So as a next step... I simply offer you... "What if?"

What if... you were willing to think about some of your BIG dreams? What if... you were willing to remember some of those things that you have always wanted to do? What if... you were willing to take some small but significant steps towards those BIG dreams?

What if?

Now, I'll be the first one to admit that it will probably take some guts, but I believe you're up to the challenge. I've seen enough real people... just like you and me... do this. They are people who have been knocked down... but they get back up... dust themselves off... and begin to think about their BIG dreams again. Just like you... they've had the courage to begin the process. And then... it happens. Their dream is ignited. That spark occurs and they take that first step. Then another. Then another. Inspiration strikes. Momentum begins. Connections happen. Doors open.

Let's face it, that's how BIG dreams get done. One small but significant step at a time.

How about it? Are you in? Are you willing to begin the process of thinking about some of your BIG dreams? I believe you are and I can't wait to journey with you as you do!

Step 1: Start dreaming

Seems pretty simple, doesn't it? We all sometimes feel like we were meant to do something more, but we don't always know where to START.

You may not know what each step of the way looks like, but give yourself permission to START dreaming BIG now!

The Intellectual Immune System ™

As we get started, I feel like I need to warn you about something. This book contains a number of stories and questions, but it doesn't offer a lot of specific answers. But… there's good reason for that. The reason can be summed up in three words.

"Intellectual Immune System™."

What is that? Well, after years of coaching and working with groups, I have a theory. It's that our intellect has an immune system similar to our body's immune system.

Much like our bodies will reject anything foreign, even if it needs it, our intellect will attack an idea because it comes from outside us.

Let me paint a picture to explain. I have a friend who needed a new kidney. His doctor explained why, so he understood the reasons for the surgery. His mom stepped up and offered to be the donor so it was a perfect match. They found a well-respected surgeon and the procedure went off without a hitch. But even though he knew he needed a new kidney, even though it was a perfect match and even though the surgery went incredibly well, what did his body do? It rejected it.

Why?

Well… it was foreign. It came from outside him. So his body's immune system kicked in and tried to shut it down.

Our intellect can do the same thing. Can't it?

Even though we may need an idea, solution or piece of advice, we tend to reject it… maybe not immediately, but over time.

Test the theory with me.

Let me ask you this: Have you ever read a book that provides six amazing principles or five new habits that you loved?

Maybe you completely connected with the author and wondered whether they had cameras in your house or workplace because they seemed to know your situation so well.

Maybe you committed to trying those new concepts but within a week you'd forgotten what principles 4, 5 and 6 were or you couldn't remember the first three habits!

Well, that was probably your Intellectual Immune System (I.I.S.) kicking in.

Even though the solution seemed to be a great fit, it came from outside you. So, over time, your I.I.S. started to work on it and attack the ideas. (I'm even betting that within a few more weeks, you were on the verge of forgetting the author's name or the title of the book.)

Have you experienced this? I'm betting you have.

Yeah… so that's the Intellectual Immune System.

It's hard to beat. But don't worry. There is a way around it.

How?

"Ownership."

That's right. Instead of me offering you an eight-step program, I will simply help you create your own solutions.

That way, you "own" it.

create
your own
solutions.

It comes from you. As a result, your Intellectual Immune System won't try to shut it down.

Now... I will still offer you some stories and ideas to inspire you.

I'll also offer some questions to guide you. But you'll create the outcome.

Again... you'll own it.

As a result, you'll be able to beat your Intellectual Immune System.

More importantly, you'll get clear on some of your BIG dreams and you'll be able to develop a plan for achieving them!

Questions to Get You Thinking

Now, before we start to get too specific about your dreams and dreaming BIG again… I need to ask you a few questions that will really help us begin our process of beating the I.I.S.

It may seem obvious, but take a minute to answer this question: Why might it be important for people to take some time to think about their goals and dreams?

_____

_____

_____

_____

_____

_____

_____

_____

_____

_____

_____

_____

_____

_____

_____

_____

_____

Hmmm...

Your Favorite People

Think about a few of the favorite people in your life. Next, think about why might it be important for them to be thinking about some of their BIG dreams?

Next, get specific. Write some of your favorite people's names down and think of a few reasons why you'd love to see them dreaming BIG right now?

Name of Favorite Person   Reason to Dream BIG right now!

NOTE: We don't do this to make you feel like you need to push people into dreaming BIG. We just do it because it's important to dream BIG *with others*. So this may simply help you think about some of the favorite people in your life and encourage *you* to encourage *them* in their BIG dreams!

Name of Favorite Person   Reason to Dream BIG right now!

_____   _____

                                           _____

                                           _____

                                           _____

_____   _____

                                           _____

                                           _____

                                           _____

                                           _____

_____   _____

                                           _____

                                           _____

                                           _____

_____   _____

                                           _____

                                           _____

                                           _____

                                           _____

What Might Happen?

By the way, here's another thought. What if you invited a few of your favorite people to walk through this process with you? What might happen if you were to dream BIG together?

_____

_____

_____

_____

_____

_____

_____

_____

_____

_____

_____

_____

_____

_____

_____

_____

_____

_____

DREAM
BIG
together

WHY
dream BIG
Now?

Why Now?

List some reasons why it might be important for you to dream BIG right now.

_____

_____

_____

_____

_____

_____

_____

_____

_____

_____

_____

_____

_____

_____

_____

_____

_____

_____

_____

_____

_____

_____

Re-sparking Dreams

A few years ago, my wife Melissa and I started something called the BIG Dream Gathering. I'd love to tell you that we did it for completely altruistic reasons but that wouldn't be true.

At the time, we were in a tough place. We had been working on one of our own BIG dreams but then we suffered a number of setbacks in a short period of time. We had a computer crash and we'd lost key files. We were having manufacturing problems with our prototype. And the kicker… we were quickly running out of money. Yup. Our BIG dream was on the ropes.

I'll admit that I was ready to give up. I was tired. I was frustrated. I was even a little sad. But as I was sitting in all of those emotions, I was reminded that we all have BIG dreams. We do, don't we? Even though many of our BIG dreams get buried or dismissed… we all have 'em.

Then I started to wonder… What if?

What could happen if we got just a few of our friends together for the express purpose of dreaming BIG together?

Maybe we could help each other. Maybe we could encourage each other. Maybe we could give each other some ideas.

OUR
BIG dream
was on
the
ropes

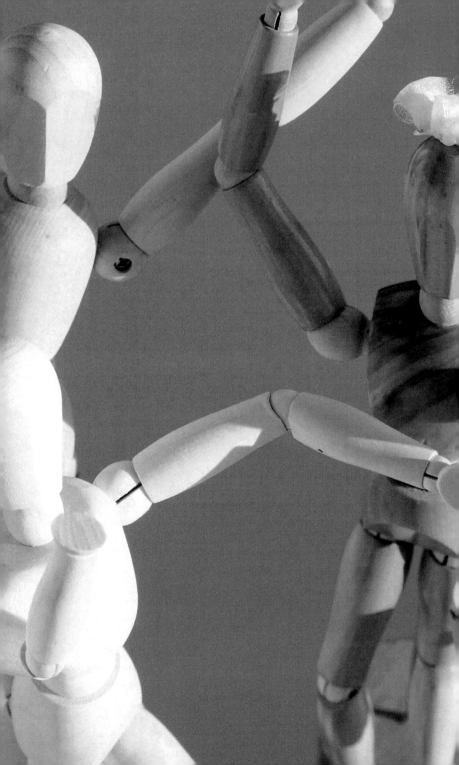

SO we decided to THROW A party

We knew that we needed a name, so in a pinch we called it the "BIG Dream Gathering."

We invited a few friends to our house on a Tuesday night. Once everyone was there we asked everyone to put some of their BIG dreams on sheets of paper and post them on our walls. Then we encouraged everyone to walk around and look at each other's dreams to see if they could help out... either by offering an encouraging word, a connection or some support.

Well... if there was any doubt that we all have dreams... the response at our first BIG Dream Gathering offered some proof.

We expected 20 people to arrive, but we had more that 30 people come that first night.

More surprisingly, we expected the gathering to last a few hours. It wound up lasting a week!

That's right. Friends who had attended the first night called to ask if they could bring others over for a second night. By the third night we had total strangers coming to the house and it just kept going! I'll admit that my wife and I were blown away by the response. We were impressed by the hoards of people that came over that week, but we were even more excited about the numerous dreams that got launched because of it.

Some people were bolstered by some encouraging words and completed books they'd wanted to write. Another person got help with a BIG dream of going to Africa to help some kids she'd read about who were living in a garbage dump. Two people even connected and eventually wound up with a contract with a major shoe company. I can't tell you which company, but if a person ran by you wearing their shoes... they'd make a "swooshing" sound!

Very real people... just like you and me... who were willing to think about some of their dreams and write them down. It was proof positive that we all have BIG dreams... and there's power when we write them down.

But here's the most important thing: Even though these BIG Dream Gatherings have continued and we've now seen thousands and thousands of people come dream BIG with us, it doesn't take a BIG Dream Gathering for you to think about your BIG dreams!

You can do it right now.

What might be some things that you'd write down?

If someone asked you... "What are a few of the things you've dreamt of doing?" What might you say?

Give it some thought. It's okay if some seem impossible. It's okay if some seem too big, too risky or too expensive.

Write them down. You don't have to have a plan yet. You don't have to know how it would work out yet. Just give it a little time... and see what comes to mind.

Use the questions and space on the following pages to think about some of your BIG dreams... and just see where it takes you.

Think Forward,
Think Back

What are a few things that you would love to do or accomplish?

What were some of the things you dreamt of doing when you were a little kid?

_____

_____

_____

_____

_____

_____

_____

_____

_____

_____

_____

_____

_____

_____

_____

_____

_____

_____

_____

_____

BIG Dreams - We All Have 'Em

Okay, in the last section, you wrote down some BIG dreams and that is great! I'm hoping it felt good to do it. As more come to mind, keep going back to record them. Have fun with it and continue to see where it takes you.

At the same time, I'm guessing that some of you maybe had some trouble. For some of you, it may have been tough. You may have felt stuck. Maybe things have been hard lately, so when you started to think about your goals and dreams, nothing came to mind. That's okay. We're with you and we're in this together.

Either way... whether you thought of so many dreams you had to grab extra paper or you sat and looked at a blank page... It's okay.

Let's simply take this next step... together.

And... I know that I border on offensive by making the following suggestion... but I'm going to do it anyway.

Go buy a lottery ticket.

Yes... a lottery ticket.

Just one will do.

Why?

Well, has anyone ever asked you what you'd do with a boatload of money?

I bet they have.

And I'm also betting you took a stab at answering it. Maybe the answer came easy or maybe it was hard. Maybe you stayed at a surface level or maybe you got specific.

go buy a
ticket!

As a life coach, I've asked similar questions of my clients to help them to dream BIG and think beyond their current situation. But I have to confess that I hadn't done this exercise personally for a long time. Recently, that all changed when my wife and I had some spare time and the need to take a drive in the country.

On our way out of town, we stopped and grabbed a lotto ticket. Then, as we drove, we just started dreaming as if our ticket had hit BIG! Sure we thought about what a dream house would look like, where we'd vacation, who we'd go and see, etc. Then we went beyond that... way beyond that. And we started to get specific!

take a mini *dream* vacation

For example, we started to dream up a non-profit that we could start. We thought about what it could achieve. We thought about whom it would help and where it would be based. Then we went further. We thought of the people who'd sit on the board, the people we'd need to walk us through the process, the specific people we'd impact. I mean we had lists of specific people and specific names!

We allowed it to get so real that we could see it actually happening. We could hear it. Smell it. Taste it!

Now, I'll admit that I'm not a huge fan of gambling. And I'm not even a big fan of lotteries... but that dollar on that night was a great investment. Not because we hit the BIG jackpot. (Cuz, we didn't.)

It was a great investment because it allowed my wife and me to take a mini-dream vacation. It blew the dust off of some of our old dreams and helped us to think of a few new ones.

We got to see a bit of our future and explore it. Plus, it left us asking the question... Why wait on the dream? Why not go for it now with or without the lottery's help!?!

That dollar and that silly little ticket allowed us to dream a little bigger, and laugh a bit more. And, with a little divine inspiration mixed in, we saw a future that excited us in BIG ways!

So maybe you don't need to buy an actual ticket. But I know for us it just made it a bit more fun... and a bit more real. Plus, I know that lotto ticket will be taped to my journal next to our notes as a $1 souvenir for our little vacation to visit the possibilities.

Consider this next set of questions and see where they take you.

What Would You Do?

So, what would be on your list, if you hit it BIG? What would you do with $10, $20 or $50 million? Again, have some fun with it and see where it takes you!

_____

_____

_____

_____

_____

_____

_____

_____

_____

_____

_____

_____

_____

_____

_____

_____

_____

_____

_____

_____

Have fun with it!

_____

_____

_____

_____

_____

_____

_____

_____

_____

_____

_____

_____

_____

_____

_____

_____

_____

_____

_____

_____

_____

Who & How Would You Impact?

If money were no object, who would be positively impacted by some of your BIG dreams? Your family? A specific group of people? A specific group of kids? A specific person?

How would it help them if your BIG dream became a reality? Go ahead. Get specific. See what happens.

_____

_____

_____

_____

_____

_____

_____

_____

_____

_____

_____

_____

_____

_____

_____

How'd You Do It?

Okay, so we've been exercising our dreaming muscle for a while. By now, you've written down a few BIG dreams, and that's great!

But chances are at least part of your brain is pondering questions like... "How would I get some of these things done?" "Where would I even start?" Or... "Who am I to do something like this?"

Well... to begin to answer some of those questions... I offer the following story.

My wife Melissa and I lived in Billings, Montana, a few years ago. When we were there, we lived in an older, established neighborhood and we had one of those neighbors. You know. The one with the perfectly manicured yard.

One day as I drove by, I noticed that neighbor had added some river rock to his perfectly sculpted landscaping.

It looked great. It was something that Melissa and I both liked. There was something about the river rock that appealed to man and woman alike. Somehow... it was rugged yet refined.

My first instinct was to think: "I like that. I want that for my yard."

My second instinct was to ponder, "How could I do this quick and cheap?" (Can you identify?)

So that next weekend, I decided to go get some rocks. I thought, "Heck, I live in Montana. Rocks are everywhere. Why not?"

The result?

I spent about five hours driving on old mountain roads looking for rock and loading them into the back of my truck. I spent $50 in gas. Plus, I had to spend $250 a few weeks later to repair the suspension on my truck. Oh, and I also I spent $8 for a bottle of Motrin to help my aching back!

All of it... for a relatively small pile of rocks.

So, what did I do next? Well, it's what I should have done first.

I decided to ask my neighbor about his rocks and how he'd done it.

Now, as I got ready to visit my neighbor, dread started to creep in. I wondered how he would react to my request for help.

I thought he might strike some sort of super hero pose with his hands boldly on his hips and a cape waving in the wind. Then I envisioned him saying, in a voice loud enough for the entire neighborhood to hear, "Ahhh ha ha, I'd be happy to help my young landscaping neighbor!"

But as it turned out, he was great. Instead of striking a super hero pose, he was gracious, thoughtful and quieter than I had imagined.

In fact, I think he was complimented that I asked.

In short order, he explained that there was a quarry outside of town and that they brought him a HUGE load of rocks for $50... in less than 24 hours!

Yes... 50 bucks... and no heavy lifting!

Wow.

What did I learn? What was the lesson my heroic neighbor offered me?

I learned that I need to always be asking the question: "Who could I be learning from?"

Then, I need to seek out those people for help.

I also learned that it sometimes helps to seek those people out BEFORE I try something new.

Again, can you identify?

As you look at your list of some of the things you're dreaming about doing, you might be thinking about making a change or wondering whether you need to try something new.

Maybe you're thinking about traveling to someplace new. Or that you want to try a new hobby or sport.

You may be thinking about a career change. Or pondering the idea of starting a new business or selling an old one.

Maybe some of you were inspired to add something to the mix... a new challenge... a new idea. You know... a new mountain to climb.

If that's the case, then why not take a next step and ask yourself the question: "Who could I learn from?"

Why not look around and see if you can find someone doing something similar to what you think you might want to do?

Then give them a call or buy them some coffee and pick their brain.

I know, I know, it's almost too simple. But if I had heeded this advice a little sooner it would have saved me some time, money, and a whole lot of back pain!

pick
someone's
brain

...A Word of Guidance

I just want to include a little guidance here.

If a person you want to connect with makes their living from what you want to talk with them about, don't just expect them to give you all their wisdom over coffee.

Seek them out and let them know your story.

But if it's appropriate... offer to pay them for their time.

Some will accept it. Some won't. Both are fine. It's up to the person.

But by offering, you're honoring them and the time that they've put into learning and developing their craft.

That's it.

It's simple but it will make a big difference in showing your respect for the person and what they've done.

honor
them
& their
time

Who's Your Hero?

In the left-hand column below, list three to five people who are doing things that interest you. What if you contacted one of them each week? What if you were able to talk with them about what they were doing and how they got started?

What might be some questions you'd want to ask them? In the right-hand column below, write down some of the questions you'd like to ask.

Person   Potential Questions to Ask

Person   Potential Questions to Ask

_____   _____

                                          _____

                                          _____

                                          _____

_____   _____

                                          _____

                                          _____

                                          _____

_____   _____

                                          _____

                                          _____

                                          _____

_____   _____

                                          _____

                                          _____

                                          _____

_____   _____

                                          _____

                                          _____

Encourage Your Heroes

One of the things you can do to also bless the people you reach out to is to encourage them. It may sound outlandish to some, but everyone needs encouragement, even if they act like they don't. That's right, even heroes need to be encouraged!

So, what's one thing that you could do to encourage each of the people you reach out to? Think about it. Is it letting them know how they have inspired you? Is it letting them know how you've seen them make an impact on the people around them? What are some specific ways that you could encourage them? List some ideas out in the space below.

Person   An Idea to Encourage Them

_____   _____

_____

_____

_____

_____   _____

_____

_____

_____   _____

_____

So offer some encouragement along the way. Your request for help and your connection may wind up blessing the person's socks off!

Even heroes
need encouragement.

Think Back...

Are you still wondering whether these people would be open to talking with you? That's fair. But… what if you asking for their insight complimented them? What if they were encouraged by your request? It's at least possible, isn't it? **Describe a time when someone asked you for help and you enjoyed the experience of assisting them.**

_____

_____

_____

_____

_____

_____

_____

_____

_____

_____

_____

_____

_____

Now, what if your request for help impacted the person you're connecting with in the same way you were touched?

What if?

Are Setbacks a "Sign"?

Recently, on the morning of some important meetings involving a BIG dream of mine, I walked out to find one of my tires was flat. I mean it was "I didn't know a tire could be that flat" flat. I have to admit that I wasn't too surprised. I'm not a Murphy's Law kind of guy, but I'm also not in the rainbows, little ponies and butterflies camp either. Things can go wrong. And they usually happen at inconvenient times. We all know this. It's not revolutionary.

But in those moments when things don't go right... it's tempting to start thinking that maybe we're wrong. And in the case of pursuing your dreams... if you hit a snag or two... it's easy to start wondering if you should go after the dream at all.

In fact, I had a friend who was like this. He could talk about his dreams with gusto, but if he ran into a obstacle or a hiccup, he would ponder if it was a sign that he should wait... or stop all together. In some cases, when I ran into set backs, he would give me advice to do the same. And... I have to admit that as I was looking at my flat-as-a-blueberry-pancake tire that morning, I began to hear this friend's voice in my head and I started to doubt.

Can you relate?

I know. I know. We don't doubt our dreams when we're well rested and well funded, but on those days when we're a little tired or a little "tight," it's just a bit easier to wonder, "Should I keep going?"

But... I'm happy to report that in the very second doubt started to creep in... another thought came racing through my mind with the speed of a stock car with four fresh tires. The thought was short and sweet. It was simple and to the point.

I simply remembered, "FLATS HAPPEN."

They do don't they? And... sometimes flats happen because you hit a nail. Not because you're doing the wrong thing. It's not an omen. It's not a sign. It's just a flat.

So remember... as you are pursuing some of your BIG dreams... FLATS HAPPEN. And when they do... grab the spare with the enthusiasm of a NASCAR pit crew and just keep going.

It'll
be
worth it!

flats HAPPEN try this one on

Step 2: Take action!

Now that you've had some practice Dreaming BIG, it's time to put your udeas to work and set them into motion. But don't worry, we don't suggest that you go it alone.

The next section helps you create an ACTION plan and think about people who might walk along side of you. You will also discover who you might help, and what might be holdind you back!

SOMETIMES YOU JUST NEED TO
Start Playing the Game

A few years ago, I attended a chess club orientation at my son's elementary school.

He was in first grade and it was his first experience with the game.

Now, I'm not going to lie. The thought of teaching a bunch of elementary school children how to play chess is a bit scary, but a couple of brave parents took the job and started to explain how it all worked.

One parent started by reviewing the rules.

He did a great job of explaining how the various pieces moved. He showed the kids how some moved forward, some moved to the side and some could go anywhere they darn well pleased.

For a while, the kids stayed with him, grasping at the rules and logistics. But then you could tell they started to get lost in everything there was to understand.

So another parent came from the back of the room and simply said, "Maybe we should just have everybody try to play the game?"

You could tell the first parent was relieved by the suggestion and the kids launched into experimenting with the various pieces.

As you can imagine, they devoured the game.

Some kids were laughing but some stared at the board with the intensity of a Russian Chess Champion.

Most made mistakes as they played, but they were learning as they went.

It was fun. It was an adventure.

Then it struck me. Sometimes we are just like these kids.

We get a new idea. We get struck by something we want to try and then we dive into the rules and the regulations. Right? It's not a bad thing.

Many times, it's the smart thing to do.

Maybe it's an idea for a new product. It would make sense to research the rules around that. It would also make sense to dig in and check out the markets, competitors and opportunities. Right?

Or, maybe it's a new career.

It would be important to check into things before making a leap. You know. Read about the industry. Talk to people who are doing it. Find out more.

BUT, just like kids getting lost in the rules of chess, sometimes we get stuck there. Don't we? Our eyes glaze over and the idea dies on the vine.

Sound familiar?

Sometimes you may just need someone to say, "It's okay. Just try."

Play.

Just set up a few boundaries.

Let's agree that maybe you shouldn't spend thousands on equipment for your new product right away, but maybe you could find someone to help you make a prototype to test with people.

Maybe you shouldn't march in and quit your job today, but maybe there's someone you could spend time with that's doing exactly what you want to be

doing. Maybe you could spend a day shadowing them to experiment and see if you really connect.

What do you think?

Here's my suggestion after watching the kids learn how to play chess and after coaching people over the years: Figure out a way to "play" today.

Try something. Have some fun. Limit the risks, but get out there and play the game.

Just like my son and his classmates, you will make some mistakes. But isn't that one of the best ways to really learn?

What to Try & Ways to Practice

So… what are a few things you could try that would give you a taste of one of your BIG dreams?

_____

_____

_____

_____

_____

_____

_____

_____

_____

_____

_____

_____

_____

_____

_____

_____

_____

_____

_____

_____

What might be some ways to "practice" one of your dreams?

_____

_____

_____

_____

_____

_____

_____

_____

_____

_____

_____

_____

_____

_____

_____

_____

_____

_____

_____

Look For Complementary Dreams

We love it when real people with "Complementary Dreams" connect.

Sometimes it happens at BIG Dream Gatherings and sometimes it happens over coffee with a friend.

What am I talking about when I say "Complementary Dreams?"

Well, these are dreams that can stand alone but they could be better... together.

These can be dreams that could help each other.

Yup... "Complementary Dreams."

Let me explain with a personal example.

Over the years, as we've held our BIG Dream Gatherings, I've had people ask for tools that would help them get clearer on their dreams and then build a plan to walk them out. They didn't want a 400-page self-help book. They simply wanted something that would allow them to take that inspiring feeling from the gathering with them... and keep moving forward in their dream journey.

So, I thought a book might be the answer. At the same time, I didn't want it to be just a book.

It may sound strange, but as I thought about it... I realized that I didn't want the reader to just read. I wanted them to have an "experience."

Now... to be honest, I wasn't entirely sure what it would look like or how I could get it done, but it became one of my BIG dreams.

Enter Jocelyn Wallace.

better together.

Jocelyn is a long-time family friend. My wife and I have always admired her spunky style and her incredible gifts.

You see, Jocelyn has come full circle in her life and career, and it's been neat to watch.

In her early years she worked as a graphic designer in an in-house agency for a major computer company. As she was recruited by other corporations over the years, opportunities led to less creative roles. But she knew she was made to do something more.

In fact, she left her corporate position to strike out on her own. Then she created a freakishly cool business infusing visual thinking into her practice as a speaker and business coach.

Did you catch it? She's blending the worlds of creativity and business. They can stand alone, but they are better together. Way better.

In short, she's just cool people. And she's got some BIG dreams.

What I didn't know is that some of her BIG dreams were complementary to mine!

As we talked about her new venture, we started to compare notes on some of our BIG dreams. I explained my BIG dream of producing a book that would be an "experience." And she relayed how she wanted to co-create a book that would break traditions and allow for the content to be pushed in a visual way.

At first, we talked about some of the ideas and stories that I wanted to relay and she immediately started to throw out concepts that I hadn't thought of before.

Then she asked to see a copy of the actual book. At that time, I had a very rough draft and I have to say that I was a little embarrassed to show her.

NET WT. 1/
(14 G)

7/10 OZ.

BOTTLED IN THE USA BY M. KAMENSTEIN, INC., E

NET WT. 3/
(9 G)

BOTTLED IN THE USA BY M. KA

NET

BOTTLED IN THE USA BY M. KA

But she was gracious and asked to see it anyway, so I sent her a copy. Then she asked if she could experiment with it. I agreed and let her fly.

Jocelyn was inspired and she quickly got to work on not only laying out the overall design, but she also created original photography for each segment and sketched ideas for additional content. She had so much fun that the ideas just flowed and the book started to come together.

I have to tell you that I wish you could have been there when we connected a week later. She'd asked to meet at a local coffee shop so she could see my reaction. I'll never forget sitting at the table with warm lattes pushed to the side.

I was excited and a little nervous.

But as she got out her initial draft and slid it across the table, my heart started to race.

I grabbed at the stack of paper and thumbed my way through. I was blown away by what she had done in such a short time. More importantly, I was struck by how the images helped my writing come alive.

Sometimes the photography represented metaphors that would support a story. Sometimes they added flavor. And sometimes the photos would make you pause and think. It was truly an experience, which is what I had asked for. But it was better than I had hoped or imagined it could be.

And that is a picture of how "Complementary Dreams" work.

Jocelyn used her BIG dream to help me with mine. And my BIG dream helped with hers.

And that was just the beginning. We continued to work together to put a plan in place to get it done! And we pushed each other and encouraged each other along the way.

And again, that's how Complementary Dreams work, too. You get to walk along side each other and help each other. You get to use your gifts, skills and dreams to help someone else achieve more with theirs.

So, yes, Complementary Dreams made it possible for you to be reading this book right now!

How cool is that? Now, I want to get you some questions to help you start thinking about this more... but before we do, I want to touch on one last thing. That is that as Jocelyn and I discussed next steps, we worked out a financial agreement that would be mutually beneficial as well.

Now, some of you may be surprised that I mention it, but it's important.

Why?

Well, sometimes it's helpful and appropriate to exchange equal work for free or at reduced fees so you can help each other to get started. And in the right seasons, that can be a wild blessing for everyone involved.

In some ways, it's a form of old school bootstrapping combined with new school BIG dreaming!

And in this day and age, when most of us don't have a lot of extra time or money, it can be a way that enables us to help each other as we move towards our BIG dreams.

However, it's also critical to not assume that Complementary Dreams will always mean that people give their skills away.

As you explore potential Complementary Dreams with someone else, figure out ways to make sure it's a win-win for everyone involved.

Sometimes that might just mean helping each other out. Sometimes that might mean figuring out ways to trade services. And... sometimes that means paying each other as you work together on those BIG dreams.

Okay. Good stuff. Enough said.

Let's get to those questions so you can be thinking about your dreams and the people around you that might have Complementary Dreams to yours.

What Does Your Dream Need?

What are some things that you still need when it comes to some of your BIG dreams?

_____

_____

_____

_____

_____

_____

_____

_____

_____

_____

_____

_____

NOTE: Your first instinct might be to think that you don't know anyone or to think that asking for help might be a burden to that person. Sure, it's a risk, but we've seen that when people are going after their BIG dreams, things tend to work out and be a gift to everyone involved! And we've seen this play out time and time again. So try putting some of those doubts aside for 10 minutes. Give it some more thought. See what you get.

Who might be someone who could help you with some of these things?

_____

_____

_____

_____

_____

_____

_____

How might you be able to help them?

_____

_____

_____

_____

_____

_____

_____

_____

_____

The Power of *3.*

Congratulations! If you've come this far... that means you've been doing some serious thinking about some of your BIG dreams. That's awesome.

More importantly... if you've had the courage to write some of them down (and I bet you have) you've taken a critical step that most people never take.

Now... it's time to start to put a plan together.

As we start this part of the discussion, I will admit that I'm a bit of a dichotomy.

I love a good plan, but at the same time, my plans have the tendency to get so complicated and intricate that I have to stop using them.

Or, I get overwhelmed and bail.

Can you relate?

So, although I love the process of building elaborate flow charts and spreadsheets, I've realized there is a danger of going over the top and rendering a plan useless.

So... the key here is going to be keeping it simple.

Agreed?

But before we move into planning mode, let me ask you this.

What would it feel like to put a plan together for your BIG dreams?

Not a 238-page plan with bar graphs and pie charts, but a simple AND applicable plan for the next six to 12 months.

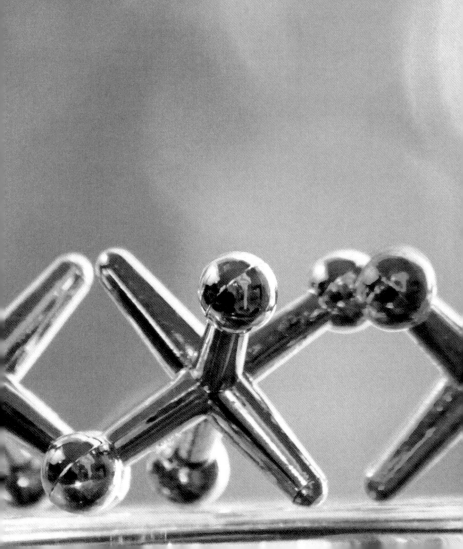

Think about it. What would it feel like to make some major strides towards your BIG dreams?

It'd probably feel pretty good. Right?

So, what if? What if we do it?

Hey... and remember... let's keep it short and to the point... okay?

That's right... since many of you are working on your BIG dreams as you are doing other things, working other jobs or navigating other responsibilities... the more simple the plan.... the better!

So... let's use the Power of 3's™... to create a simple but powerful plan!

Here are some "power of 3" questions for you to ponder...

Power of 3: Narrow Your Focus

For this next session, it will help to get specific. So I'm going to ask you to narrow your focus to one dream or set of dreams. That will allow you to put a set of specific steps together for that dream. Know that you can walk through this "Power of 3" process with multiple dreams and goals, but it helps to do it one at a time. So let's start there.

Take a look back through all of the dreams and goals that you've written down so far. Now in the space below, write down the three that stand out to you as the ones that you want to get started on soon.

_____

_____

_____

_____

_____

Now, out of these three pick one (that's right—one), and write it down here. This is the one we'll build the first plan for. (Go ahead. Write it down. You can do it!)

_____

_____

_____

_____

_____

_____

What are three things you'd like to accomplish for this dream in the next six to 12 months?

_____

_____

_____

_____

_____

_____

_____

_____

_____

_____

_____

_____

_____

_____

When would you love to accomplish these things? (That's right. Why not assign some dates to these accomplishments?)

#1 _____   Date: _____

#2 _____   Date: _____

#3 _____   Date: _____

Power of 3:
People Questions

Who are three people (or types of people) who will be impacted by this dream?
These might be people with Complementary Dreams or they might be people
who would benefit from these dreams being realized.

_____

_____

_____

_____

_____

_____

_____

_____

_____

_____

_____

_____

_____

_____

_____

_____

_____

_____

_____

What are three ways you can reach out to these people to get them excited about... or involved in... this BIG dream?

_____

_____

_____

_____

_____

_____

_____

_____

_____

_____

_____

_____

_____

_____

_____

_____

_____

_____

_____

Power of 3:
Money Questions

Here's another set that involve money. I know... I know... this might be a tender subject... but I'll ask them anyway.

What are three things that you may need to spend money on for your BIG dream in the next six to 12 months?

_____

_____

_____

_____

_____

_____

_____

_____

_____

_____

_____

_____

_____

_____

_____

_____

_____

_____

What are three ways that you could possibly bring in or save some extra money to help pay for those things? (Go ahead. Get creative on this! See where your imagination takes you!)

_____

_____

_____

_____

_____

_____

_____

_____

_____

_____

_____

_____

_____

_____

That's it for now.

Sure, we could go further... but if you answer these Power of 3 questions, you'll have the beginnings of a solid AND simple plan for your BIG dream for the next six to 12 months!

What My Dog Taught Me
ABOUT BIG DREAMS

Okay. So, we've been thinking about some of our BIG dreams and goals. We've been coming up with plans to start walking them out, and we've been thinking about the people who could help us and who we could help in the process.

It's exciting. It's inspiring. And it can even be a little scary.

We've taken these steps and you're getting ready to take some more.

But before we do, I want to share a lesson from my dog.

See... we have a really smart dog. Her name is Lilly.

She's an Australian Shepherd, which means she's been bred to herd sheep and anticipate her owner's every need.

Seriously, she's wicked smart. She's so smart that she not only responds to voice commands, but also watches you and responds to a quick hand signal.

In fact, she's so intelligent that sometimes when she is looking at me, I get a sense that she's figuring out how much smarter she is than me!

Now, what's interesting is that even though she's brilliant, she has "learned" something that is obviously false.

When we first got her she was tiny. And due to her size, she had trouble going up and down the stairs to our basement. So I'd carry her. This continued for the first few months of her life.

Then something interesting happened.

In that time, she "learned" that she couldn't go up and down those stairs.

It's really curious to watch because she will climb any other stairs on the planet. She'll climb the stairs at the park, the stairs at Nana and Papa's house and the stairs at the school across the street. But she won't go up or down the stairs to our basement.

I'm not kidding. Melissa and our boys are her favorite people on the planet. She'd follow them through a forest fire if need be, but if they head to the basement to get something, she'll just stand at the top of the stairs and wait.

She's "learned" that she can't go up and down those stairs.

Is it true? Nope. Does it limit her? Yup.

As I sat and watched this phenomenon recently, I started to wonder...

What are some things that I've "learned" about myself that are totally wrong? Where have I learned limits that really don't exist?

Now, let me ask, what might be some things that you have "learned" about yourself that are totally wrong?

What if some of those false beliefs are keeping us from our BIG dreams?

It's possible, isn't it?

I'll give you an example that can further illustrate this.

Recently, one of my coaching clients wanted to start her own business. She had a great idea as well as a lot of energy and enthusiasm to back it up. She even had enough funding to get started. But she said, "I just don't get accounting and I'm worried that I'll screw things up."

She was locked up. She was stuck.

In some ways, she was Lilly standing at the top of the steps.

Why?

Well, when we probed a bit deeper, we found out that those beliefs were based on a bad experience in a high school accounting class and a belief that she would need to handle her own books as opposed to finding an awesome accountant to walk along side her.

Once she realized these "learned" beliefs were possibly wrong, she was able to think of some solutions to help her break through that belief.

Then she was able to take some very real steps toward her dream.

How about you? What might be something that you've "learned" that's both wrong AND keeping you from moving towards your BIG dream?

Did someone ever tell you, "You can't make money doing THAT"? And for whatever reason, you believed them?

Did something you try fail? So, consciously or subconsciously, you decided that you'd always fail.

Did you hear someone say that it's too late to start a new career and somehow that stuck with you? And even though you'd love to try something different, it seems impossible.

Did you try for a promotion once and not get the position? Has that experience "taught you" not to try again?

Here's a question: What if you "unlearned" a few of those things and started moving towards those BIG dreams today?

Learned Fears

Think about it. What's an example of something someone "learned" that wasn't true? How did they break through it?

_____

_____

_____

_____

_____

_____

_____

_____

_____

_____

_____

_____

_____

_____

_____

_____

_____

_____

_____

_____

What might be some things that you're afraid of in regards to some of your dreams and goals? Is it possible that those things have been "learned" but aren't true? Describe what it might feel like to break through one of those things.

_____

_____

_____

_____

_____

_____

_____

_____

_____

As an aside, if you are wondering whether we are going to teach Lilly to go up and down the basement stairs, the answer is, "Heck no!" The basement is now the oasis for our two cats. At their firm request, Lilly will stay upstairs.

What will you do today?

I recently heard a riddle that I liked.

It went like this.

There were five birds sitting on a wire.

Three decided to fly off.

How many birds were left sitting on the wire?

Go ahead... think about it. I'll give you a minute.

The answer: Five.

Because deciding to do something and actually doing it are entirely different things.

So... what is something... small but significant... that you can DO to make progress towards one of your BIG dreams today?

Don't just decide to do it.

GO DO IT !

Notes:

Step 3: Sustain your dream!

When you Dream BIG, you can expect to have a few setbacks. Sometimes you might find yourself wondering if you are on the right track. That's normal.

The third step in dreaming BIG is to protect and SUSTAIN your dream. Know when you might need a boost, give up the right things, and figure out who you can help too!

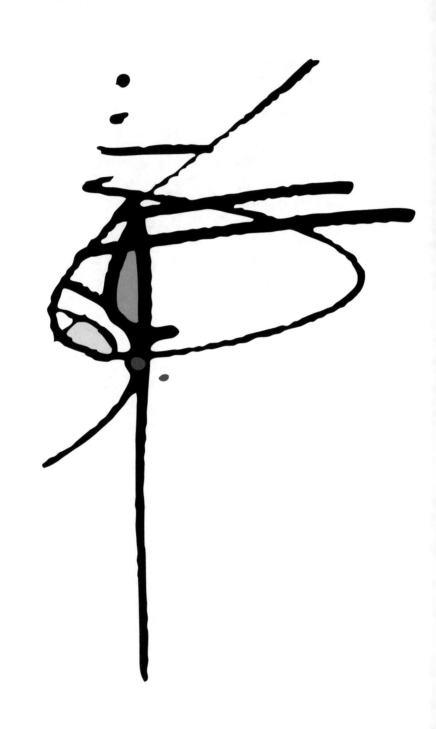

Protect Your Dream

Have you ever had someone close to you tell you that you can't go after a dream?

Maybe they were trying to protect you from getting hurt. Maybe they were afraid you'd move away if your dream happened. Maybe they were a little scared that your dream would change their world?

Whatever the reason, when someone tries to shut down a dream, it's usually not with horrible intentions but it can have horrible consequences.

No matter what: you've got to protect the dream.

How can you do it?

Here's one way: What if you surrounded yourself with at least two or three people who believe in your dream too?

I do this. First of all, I can say that I'm freakishly blessed because my wife is hugely encouraging of my dreams.

But I'm also intentional about this. One specific thing that I do is meet with three like-minded guys from the business world every other week (some call this a "Mastermind Group").

We push each other and we pray for each other. We laugh a lot and we encourage each other. We know each other and know each other's BIG dreams. We're for each other and we help each other.

For example, I will let these guys know about a specific dream or goal. I'll let them know the basics of my plan to get there and the milestones that I want to hit as I move forward.

who
helps keep
you
going?

They will ask me questions to help me get even more clear on my end goal. They'll also push me... sometimes to think or dream a little bigger. And they'll make suggestions that might help along the way.

Then I'll give these guys permission to hold me accountable to the plan as I start to walk it out, and I can trust that they'll do it in a way that will both encourage me and stretch me.

I'll say that there are days when these three guys believe in me and my dreams more than I do... and that has made all the difference.

I'll admit that it's tough for all of us to block out this time in our busy schedules but it has been so worth it.

Who are two to three people in your life who you could meet with on a regular basis with the intent purpose of encouraging each other?

The cool thing is that you don't need to be similar to these people. In fact, it might be helpful to come from diverse backgrounds and be wildly different from each other. The key is that you are like-minded in your purpose for gathering on a regular basis and encouraging each other.

Think about it. Be intentional about it. Experiment with it. (Know that it might take some time to get the right group of people.) But know that when you do, it can make all the difference!

encourage
each
other

Who are two to three people that you'd love to meet with regularly, in order to encourage and push each other to go after your dreams?

_____

_____

_____

_____

_____

_____

_____

_____

_____

_____

_____

_____

_____

_____

_____

_____

_____

_____

_____

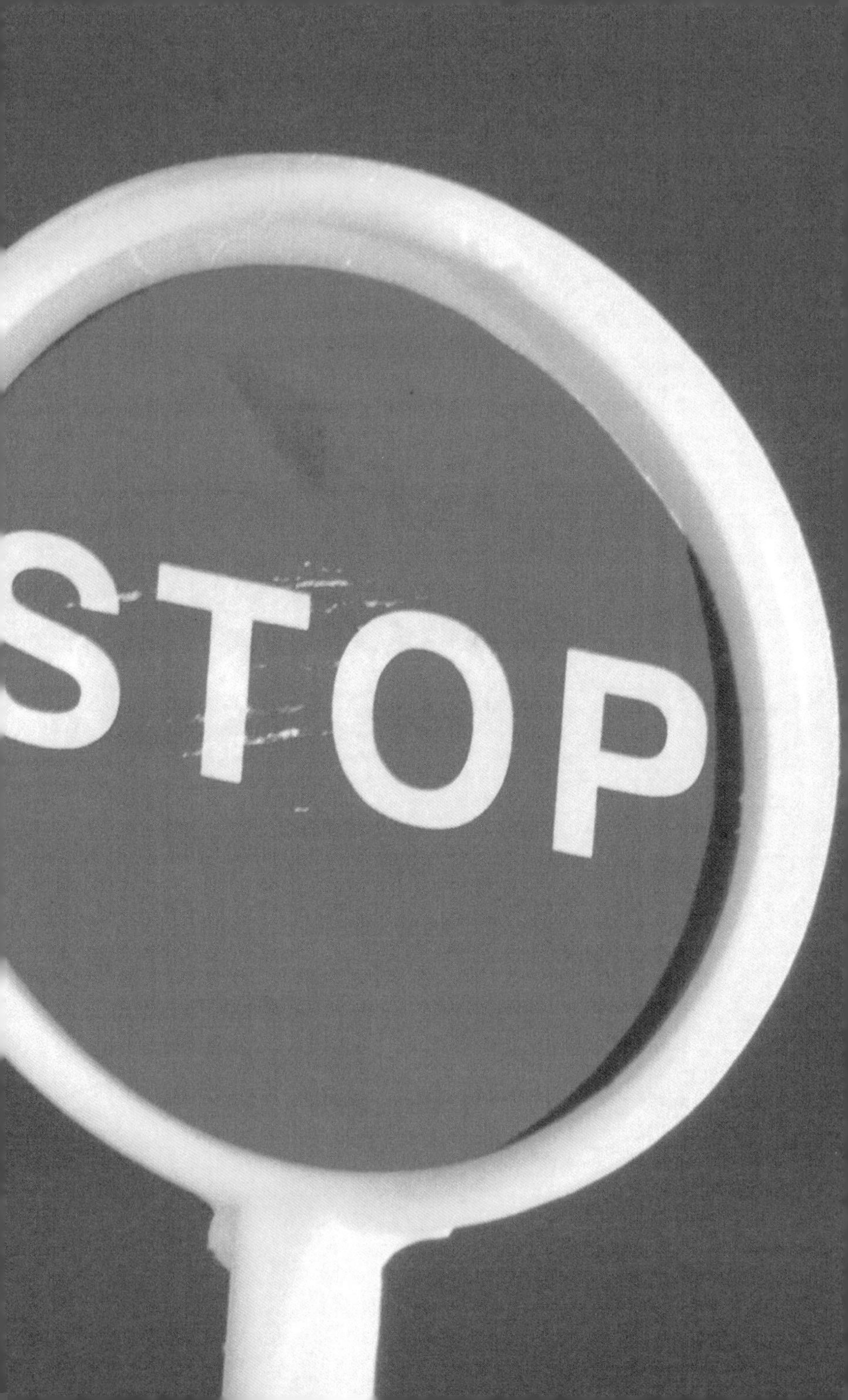
STOP

What Do You Need to Stop Doing?

Apple's Steve Jobs once said, "I'm as proud of what we don't do as I am of what we do."

Now that's a simple but powerful concept. And it definitely applies to where we are in this process.

Sometimes, as we go after our BIG dreams, instead of having to do something we have to stop doing something.

That's right. We have to quit something.

It's different for all of us and I don't know what it might be for you.

But I'm betting you might have some ideas.

Need more encouragement on this front?

Try this wisdom from Seth Godin and his book called The Dip:

Most of the time, we deal with the obstacles by persevering. Sometimes we get discouraged and turn to inspirational writing, like stuff from Vince Lombardi: "Quitters never win and winners never quit." Bad advice. Winners quit all the time. They just quit the right stuff at the right time.

Lastly, from what I've heard, America's favorite gymnast Shawn Johnson was a pretty good swimmer. It also sounds like she was a solid softball player too. But she had to choose to give those things up in order to go after the gold in gymnastics.

Give it some thought. Then maybe, just maybe, give something up.

More Time for Your BIG Dream

What's one thing that you might need to give up? Maybe it's something that you need to cut out of your schedule.

Maybe it's a hobby or TV show. What is something that you could eliminate that would give you a little extra time to work on your BIG dreams?

_____

_____

_____

_____

_____

_____

_____

_____

_____

_____

_____

_____

_____

_____

_____

_____

_____

_____

How High Do You Want to Go?

I recently volunteered during a summer festival my church was hosting. It included all things BBQ and inflatable!

On that hot July evening, I found myself at the base of one of those Velcro® walls.

Yes. I said Velcro wall. The kind of amusements where kids and adults zip into a jumpsuit made of Velcro, climb up on to a big pillow of air, jump a few times and then try to STICK themselves as high as they can.

It's a lot of fun. But I have to admit that for most folks the pillow of air and the jump didn't always work well together. Most participants looked more like Chevy Chase than Shawn Johnson as they tried to touch the sky!

The problem was that I was the volunteer up next to the wall. So, I stood on that same pillow of air trying to remain upright while helping the kids go in the right direction and attach themselves to the wall.

It took me a little while to figure out my "system," but as the evening progressed I developed a way to help the kids get as high as they could. (I'll admit that I passed on helping the heavyset middle-aged man that stepped up and looked at me with expectant eyes!)

As they'd step up to the wall, I'd have the kids practice jumping a couple of times. That would let them get a feel for their own "bounce." Then, I'd tell them on their third bounce that I'd give 'em a boost if they wanted it.

99.9995% of the kids accepted my offer.

So, first, I'd ask, "How high do you want to go? Middle-high, high-high or over-the-top?"

need a little help
with your
bounce ?

Some kids would look at me with eyes of caution and some with the eyes of Evel Knievel.

Then, once we got clear on "middle-high, high-high or over-the-top," then I'd explain the next step in the process.

I'd say, "We're going to bounce three times and on the third bounce I'm going to give you a boost. But I still need you to jump as high and as hard as you can. I'll just help you up the wall."

Once we made our adventurous pact, I'd grab the back of their Velcro suit. We'd bounce three times. Then they'd jump with all their might and I'd toss with all mine.

They would wind up either "middle-high" or "high-high" depending on their request.

(NO, we didn't have any make it over the top, although my youngest son came dangerously close!)

As you can imagine, it was a lot of fun.

The kids would "stick." They'd laugh or look around in wide-eyed amazement. Some of the parents even offered me bribes to keep their kids on the wall for an extra five minutes!

After a few hours of volunteering, I finally came down from my perch on the wall. Gradually I made my way to a cup of lemonade and a shade tree.

As I sat I realized, that Velcro wall is a picture for life. Isn't it?

I mean, we can all "jump" on our own. We can walk out our daily lives. We can work. We can even try new things. And some days we look like Chevy and some days we look like Shawn.

But when it comes down to it, in order to get to any kind of "middle-high" or "high-high" goals, we need help. Don't we?

We need to jump as hard as we can, but it helps exponentially to have someone there to give us a "boost" and help us up the "wall."

So we "stick."

Then, we'll be able to see things we never thought possible.

WHO COULD YOU HELP
Stick to New Heights?

So, here's my "Velcro Wall Challenge" to you today and really give it some thought.

Who could you give a "boost" to today?

_____

_____

_____

Who could you ask about their goals (either at home or at work)? Is it a co-worker? A friend? A neighbor? Your significant other?

Who could it be?

Think about it and write down some names.

Think about when you want to intentionally reach out to them. Ask 'em about what they want to do.

Where they want to go.

How high they want to jump.

Then ask 'em how you might be able to give 'em a boost.

Maybe it's through some connections. Maybe it's through giving some time on a Saturday afternoon. Maybe it's just calling with some encouragement for that goal once a week.

Try it.

Not with everyone, but with whomever comes to mind. And then see what happens.

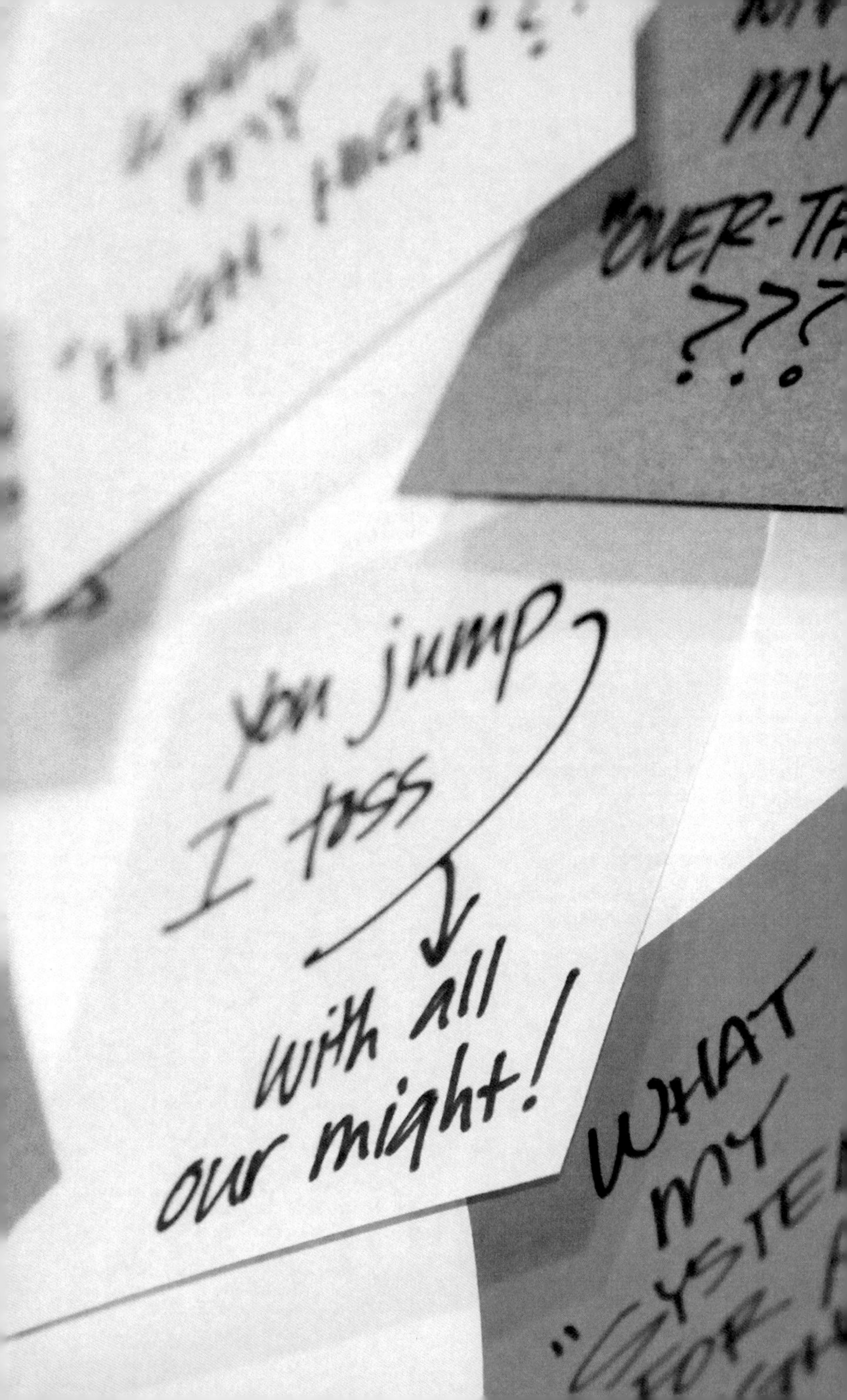
You jump
I toss
with all
our might!
WHAT
MY

And just watch. As you give some help… when you offer a little "boost" to someone else... just see what that does for you.

It might take some effort. It might take some time.

But, as you see your friend, your co-worker or your spouse "stick" to heights they didn't think were possible, notice what it does in you. I'm betting it will feel great!

And don't be surprised to feel someone else grab the back of your own "Velcro suit" in the process and start to count down... 3... 2... 1...

JUMP!

Take the challenge. Just see what happens.

Remember, we were built for BIG dreams, but we weren't built to go after them alone.

Some of your BIG dreams were meant to have an impact on a few people and some of your dreams might impact the entire world.

See what happens when you begin to go after them and help as many other dreamers along the way!

What Can NASA Teach Us?

According to NASA, the space shuttle spends most of its fuel breaking out of the earth's orbit.

Once it's free from the earth's gravitational pull... it takes a lot less energy to sustain the shuttle's heading.

Yes. The first step in the shuttle's mission takes a vast amount of energy but then it's free to explore and do what it was created to do.

Hmmmmmm.

What can this teach us about dreaming BIG?

What if we were able to break out of some of our current "orbits?"

What if we were able to break free from some of the gravitational pull of our old habits or old thinking?

What if?

What if you launched one of your BIG dreams?

It might take some energy. It might take a boost. It will definitely take a catalyst.

But what if?

Think about it... today.

What are some of the things that you want to be shooting for?

What are some of your BIG dreams?

What if you started to move towards launching one of your BIG dreams...today?`

From Bikes to BIG Dreams

As we are wrapping up this book… I want to bring you back to the bike shop I mentioned in the opening chapter… that hole-in-the-wall wonderland were I spent much of my youth.

If you remember the story, you know that at 13 I was getting to live my BIG dream.

At that time I loved the bikes, I loved the stuff, I loved the smells, I loved my coworkers and I loved our customers.

Yup… I loved the whole experience except for one thing.

As I started to walk out this dream I quickly realized that I was terrible at actually working on bikes.

I'm not kidding. I was almost dangerous.

Sure… I could put a kid's single-speed bike together with relative ease but anything beyond that and I was an OSHA hazard!

The bike shop staff was encouraging but I could also tell that everybody cringed whenever I picked up a wrench or stood within 10 feet of the workbench.

As you can imagine this was an issue.

I could tell you the merits of cantilever over caliper brakes and explain why you may want to upgrade. But if I was the one working on your brakes you might want to up your life insurance policy!

I could explain why you should consider spending $200 more for a better set of wheels. But if I was the one putting them on your bike, you'd want to limit your rides to a two-mile radius around the local hospital!

So, even though a big part of my 13-year-old dream was playing out... it wasn't playing out how I'd planned.

I could see my limitations and frankly I got nervous. Everybody started out at the shop as a mechanic. Work the wrench a bit and then you'd earn the right to move out to the sales floor.

This applied to me too. Or so I thought.

In a pinch on a busy Saturday I had to leave the workbench and hit the show room to help with a customer.

Imagine it.

There he was... a tall, middle-aged man in shorts and a T-shirt. He had his back to me and he was looking at a wall filled with handlebar bags.

There I was... a nervous 13-year-old kid who had studied every square inch of that wall. Heck, I'd spent the past two years getting to know every zipper, color and size. I knew which material had been tested by NASA and which was being used by the top racers in Italy!

So, even though I was a little scared, I approached him to see if I could help.

As it turned out, he had a pretty simple question and I answered it rather quickly.

But then I surprised myself by asking him a question.

At first, I just asked him a little bit about where he was riding. He answered.

I quickly figured out we had ridden the same roads. So we started to compare notes. We talked about the rogue farm dog and the big nasty hills. We talked

about another highway with narrow shoulders and busy traffic. We whispered about rumors of a local nature trail and boldly celebrated the glory of a long summer ride.

Then something in me just clicked.

One question led to another question. And before I knew it this man who had come in with questions about a $20 bag was leaving with a $400 bike!

I can honestly say that I'm not sure who was more surprised… the middle-aged customer or 13-year-old me!

With this newfound groove, I quickly made an agreement with the bike shop owner that I'd stay away from the workbench as much as possible and keep my feet firmly planted on the sales floor.

I committed to learning what I could there and help the rest of the staff to do the same!

On that busy Saturday, I found my home… the sweet spot of my 13-year-old domain!

Even though my BIG dream journey started out bumpy, it eventually led me to something better. In fact, it led me to another BIG dream all together.

Sure, I kept selling bikes and loving the process.

But then… one love led to another.

At first, I started out loving the bikes and, as a result, I loved to tell people about them. Gradually, however, I started to enjoy the process of asking questions and filling a need even more.

Sure, as a teenager, I still rode bikes but instead of studying bike magazines and supplier catalogs non-stop, I found myself fascinated with dorky stuff like figuring out how people learn, uncovering ways to ask better questions and finding ways to help people feel comfortable.

I will tell you that this kind of stuff didn't make me very cool in high school but I loved it. And I got pretty darn good at it.

And gradually… learning about and teaching these kinds of things became a new BIG dream.

In fact, at age 20, I held my first official two-day seminar on that same bike shop sales floor. That's right. After heading off to college, the bike shop owner asked me to come back to help his new staff with their selling skills.

I jumped at the chance. This was becoming a part of my new BIG dream, so I went all out. I taught about selling skills but we also talked about attitude. We dove into the power of asking questions but we also discussed the importance of mindset. I even hired actors to pose as customers so the team could practice!

It was fun. I was hooked. And yes… it became a big part of my next BIG dream.

A few years later, I graduated from college and continued my learning process by going into sales. Later I went into corporate training and then eventually I went on to launch my own training company with my wife.

And that's where I'm at today. But did you catch it?

I bet you did.

That's right. Our company isn't a bike shop.

Even though my dream journey started by wanting to have my own hole-in-the-wall store filled with spokes, bags and bicycles, it didn't play out that way.

It played out better.

That's right. Even though I don't have a bike shop, I still have a little chunk of heaven. I just had to start. Then take action. And finally... sustain my dream.

So think about it.

Where might your BIG dream journey take you?

Where might that next BIG dream pursuit lead you?

Sure, it might be different than you expect... but what if it's better?

I bet it will be.

Why not try?

Get to it.

And please, please, please... let us know how it goes!

Notes:

IGNITE
Dream Update Journal

We wanted to inspire you to continue IGNITING your dreams in the days and weeks to come! This Dream Update Journal will provide you a space to keep track of your dreams, the actions your taking and the strategies you're using to sustain your dreams.

We've provided you 52 pages, so you can keep track of your progress for a full year!

Simply start by writing in the date of your first week and then use the weekly questions to guide you. It might seem like it needs to be more complicated than this, but if I've learned anything it's that:

"BIG dreams are achieved by people who are willing to take small but significant steps... consistently."

So... keep dreaming BIG. Keep taking action. Keep sustaining your dreams (and the dreams of others)!

I believe in you,

Mitch

> *You don't have to see the whole staircase.*
> *Just take the first step.*
>
> MARTIN LUTHER KING, JR.

WEEK 1: _____ [DATE]

STEP 1: START (KEEP) DREAMING

List 1 dream you want to take a step towards this week and describe why it's important to you:

_____

_____

_____

STEP 2: TAKE ACTION

List at least 1 small but significant step you want to take towards this dream this week:

_____

_____

_____

STEP 3: SUSTAIN YOUR DREAMS

What's 1 small but significant thing you want to do to sustain your dream this week? (e.g. meet w/ someone, stop doing something, give someone a boost)

_____

_____

_____

> *All our dreams can come true, if we have*
> *the courage to pursue them.*
>
> WALT DISNEY

WEEK 2: _____ [DATE]

STEP 1: START (KEEP) DREAMING

List 1 dream you want to take a step towards this week and describe why it's important to you:

_____

_____

_____

STEP 2: TAKE ACTION

List at least 1 small but significant step you want to take towards this dream this week:

_____

_____

_____

STEP 3: SUSTAIN YOUR DREAMS

What's 1 small but significant thing you want to do to sustain your dream this week? (e.g. meet w/ someone, stop doing something, give someone a boost)

_____

_____

_____

> *Somebody should tell us, right at the start of our lives, that we are dying. Then we might live life to the limit, every minute of every day. Do it! I say. Whatever you want to do, do it now! There are only so many tomorrows.*
>
> POPE PAUL VI

WEEK 3: _____ [DATE]

STEP 1: START (KEEP) DREAMING

List 1 dream you want to take a step towards this week and describe why it's important to you:

_____

_____

_____

STEP 2: TAKE ACTION

List at least 1 small but significant step you want to take towards this dream this week:

_____

_____

_____

STEP 3: SUSTAIN YOUR DREAMS

What's 1 small but significant thing you want to do to sustain your dream this week? (e.g. meet w/ someone, stop doing something, give someone a boost)

_____

_____

_____

> *The man who never makes mistakes loses a*
> *great many chances to learn something.*
>
> THOMAS EDISON

WEEK 4: _____ [DATE]

STEP 1: START (KEEP) DREAMING

List 1 dream you want to take a step towards this week and describe why it's important to you:

_____

_____

_____

STEP 2: TAKE ACTION

List at least 1 small but significant step you want to take towards this dream this week:

_____

_____

_____

STEP 3: SUSTAIN YOUR DREAMS

What's 1 small but significant thing you want to do to sustain your dream this week? (e.g. meet w/ someone, stop doing something, give someone a boost)

_____

_____

_____

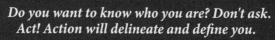

> *Do you want to know who you are? Don't ask.*
> *Act! Action will delineate and define you.*
> THOMAS JEFFERSON

WEEK 5: _____ [DATE]

STEP 1: START (KEEP) DREAMING

List 1 dream you want to take a step towards this week and describe why it's important to you:

_____

_____

_____

STEP 2: TAKE ACTION

List at least 1 small but significant step you want to take towards this dream this week:

_____

_____

_____

STEP 3: SUSTAIN YOUR DREAMS

What's 1 small but significant thing you want to do to sustain your dream this week? (e.g. meet w/ someone, stop doing something, give someone a boost)

_____

_____

_____

> *It's not about what you tell your children, but*
> *how you show them how to live life.*
>
> JADA PINKETT SMITH

WEEK 6: _____ [DATE]

STEP 1: START (KEEP) DREAMING

List 1 dream you want to take a step towards this week and describe why it's important to you:

_____

_____

_____

STEP 2: TAKE ACTION

List at least 1 small but significant step you want to take towards this dream this week:

_____

_____

_____

STEP 3: SUSTAIN YOUR DREAMS

What's 1 small but significant thing you want to do to sustain your dream this week? (e.g. meet w/ someone, stop doing something, give someone a boost)

_____

_____

_____

> *Fall seven times; stand up eight.*
>
> JAPANESE PROVERB

WEEK 7: _____ [DATE]

STEP 1: START (KEEP) DREAMING

List 1 dream you want to take a step towards this week and describe why it's important to you:

_____

_____

_____

STEP 2: TAKE ACTION

List at least 1 small but significant step you want to take towards this dream this week:

_____

_____

_____

STEP 3: SUSTAIN YOUR DREAMS

What's 1 small but significant thing you want to do to sustain your dream this week? (e.g. meet w/ someone, stop doing something, give someone a boost)

_____

_____

_____

> *We all have dreams. But in order to make dreams come into reality, it takes an awful lot of determination, dedication, self-discipline, and effort.*
>
> JESSE OWENS

WEEK 8: _____ [DATE]

STEP 1: START (KEEP) DREAMING

List 1 dream you want to take a step towards this week and describe why it's important to you:

_____

_____

_____

STEP 2: TAKE ACTION

List at least 1 small but significant step you want to take towards this dream this week:

_____

_____

_____

STEP 3: SUSTAIN YOUR DREAMS

What's 1 small but significant thing you want to do to sustain your dream this week? (e.g. meet w/ someone, stop doing something, give someone a boost)

_____

_____

_____

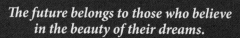

> *The future belongs to those who believe
> in the beauty of their dreams.*
>
> ELEANOR ROOSEVELT

WEEK 9: _____ [DATE]

STEP 1: START (KEEP) DREAMING

List 1 dream you want to take a step towards this week and describe why it's important to you:

_____

_____

_____

STEP 2: TAKE ACTION

List at least 1 small but significant step you want to take towards this dream this week:

_____

_____

_____

STEP 3: SUSTAIN YOUR DREAMS

What's 1 small but significant thing you want to do to sustain your dream this week? (e.g. meet w/ someone, stop doing something, give someone a boost)

_____

_____

_____

> *Every great dream begins with a dreamer. Always remember, you have within you the strength, the patience, and the passion to reach for the stars to change the world.*
>
> MARTIN LUTHER KING, JR.

WEEK 10: _____ [DATE]

STEP 1: START (KEEP) DREAMING

List 1 dream you want to take a step towards this week and describe why it's important to you:

_____

_____

_____

STEP 2: TAKE ACTION

List at least 1 small but significant step you want to take towards this dream this week:

_____

_____

_____

STEP 3: SUSTAIN YOUR DREAMS

What's 1 small but significant thing you want to do to sustain your dream this week? (e.g. meet w/ someone, stop doing something, give someone a boost)

_____

_____

_____

> *You can't have a better tomorrow if you are thinking about yesterday all the time.*
>
> CHARLES KETTERING

WEEK 11: _____ [DATE]

STEP 1: START (KEEP) DREAMING

List 1 dream you want to take a step towards this week and describe why it's important to you:

_____

_____

_____

STEP 2: TAKE ACTION

List at least 1 small but significant step you want to take towards this dream this week:

_____

_____

_____

STEP 3: SUSTAIN YOUR DREAMS

What's 1 small but significant thing you want to do to sustain your dream this week? (e.g. meet w/ someone, stop doing something, give someone a boost)

_____

_____

_____

> *There are risks and costs to action. But they are far less than the long range risks of comfortable inaction.*
>
> JOHN F. KENNEDY

WEEK 12: _____ [DATE]

STEP 1: START (KEEP) DREAMING

List 1 dream you want to take a step towards this week and describe why it's important to you:

_____

_____

_____

STEP 2: TAKE ACTION

List at least 1 small but significant step you want to take towards this dream this week:

_____

_____

_____

STEP 3: SUSTAIN YOUR DREAMS

What's 1 small but significant thing you want to do to sustain your dream this week? (e.g. meet w/ someone, stop doing something, give someone a boost)

_____

_____

_____

> *Success comes from taking the initiative and following up... persisting... eloquently expressing the depth of your love. What simple action could you take today to produce a new momentum toward success in your life?*
>
> TONY ROBBINS

WEEK 13: _____ [DATE]

STEP 1: START (KEEP) DREAMING

List 1 dream you want to take a step towards this week and describe why it's important to you:

_____

_____

_____

STEP 2: TAKE ACTION

List at least 1 small but significant step you want to take towards this dream this week:

_____

_____

_____

STEP 3: SUSTAIN YOUR DREAMS

What's 1 small but significant thing you want to do to sustain your dream this week? (e.g. meet w/ someone, stop doing something, give someone a boost)

_____

_____

_____

> *The purpose of human life is to serve, and to show compassion and the will to help others.*
>
> ALBERT SCHWEITZER

WEEK 14: _____ [DATE]

STEP 1: START (KEEP) DREAMING

List 1 dream you want to take a step towards this week and describe why it's important to you:

_____

_____

_____

STEP 2: TAKE ACTION

List at least 1 small but significant step you want to take towards this dream this week:

_____

_____

_____

STEP 3: SUSTAIN YOUR DREAMS

What's 1 small but significant thing you want to do to sustain your dream this week? (e.g. meet w/ someone, stop doing something, give someone a boost)

_____

_____

_____

> *Action is the foundational key to all success.*
> PABLO PICASSO

WEEK 15: _____ [DATE]

STEP 1: START (KEEP) DREAMING

List 1 dream you want to take a step towards this week and describe why it's important to you:

_____

_____

_____

STEP 2: TAKE ACTION

List at least 1 small but significant step you want to take towards this dream this week:

_____

_____

_____

STEP 3: SUSTAIN YOUR DREAMS

What's 1 small but significant thing you want to do to sustain your dream this week? (e.g. meet w/ someone, stop doing something, give someone a boost)

_____

_____

_____

> *If one advances confidently in the direction of his dreams,*
> *and endeavors to live the life which he has imagined, he*
> *will meet with a success unexpected in common hours.*
>
> HENRY DAVID THOREAU

WEEK 16: _____ [DATE]

STEP 1: START (KEEP) DREAMING

List 1 dream you want to take a step towards this week and describe why it's important to you:

_____

_____

_____

STEP 2: TAKE ACTION

List at least 1 small but significant step you want to take towards this dream this week:

_____

_____

_____

STEP 3: SUSTAIN YOUR DREAMS

What's 1 small but significant thing you want to do to sustain your dream this week? (e.g. meet w/ someone, stop doing something, give someone a boost)

_____

_____

_____

> *Hold fast to dreams, for if dreams die, life is*
> *a broken-winged bird that cannot fly.*
>
> LANGSTON HUGHES

WEEK 17: _____ [DATE]

STEP 1: START (KEEP) DREAMING

List 1 dream you want to take a step towards this week and describe why it's important to you:

_____

_____

_____

STEP 2: TAKE ACTION

List at least 1 small but significant step you want to take towards this dream this week:

_____

_____

_____

STEP 3: SUSTAIN YOUR DREAMS

What's 1 small but significant thing you want to do to sustain your dream this week? (e.g. meet w/ someone, stop doing something, give someone a boost)

_____

_____

_____

> *You gotta have a dream. If you don't have a dream,*
> *how you gonna make a dream come true?*
>
> OSCAR HAMMERSTEIN II

WEEK 18: _____ [DATE]

STEP 1: START (KEEP) DREAMING

List 1 dream you want to take a step towards this week and describe why it's important to you:

_____

_____

_____

STEP 2: TAKE ACTION

List at least 1 small but significant step you want to take towards this dream this week:

_____

_____

_____

STEP 3: SUSTAIN YOUR DREAMS

What's 1 small but significant thing you want to do to sustain your dream this week? (e.g. meet w/ someone, stop doing something, give someone a boost)

_____

_____

_____

All human beings are also dream beings.
Dreaming ties all mankind together.

JACK KEROUAC

WEEK 19: _____ [DATE]

STEP 1: START (KEEP) DREAMING

List 1 dream you want to take a step towards this week and describe why it's important to you:

_____

_____

_____

STEP 2: TAKE ACTION

List at least 1 small but significant step you want to take towards this dream this week:

_____

_____

_____

STEP 3: SUSTAIN YOUR DREAMS

What's 1 small but significant thing you want to do to sustain your dream this week? (e.g. meet w/ someone, stop doing something, give someone a boost)

_____

_____

_____

> *When you remove the risk, you remove the challenge.*
> *When you remove the challenge, you wither on the vine.*
>
> ALEX LOWE

WEEK 20: _____ [DATE]

STEP 1: START (KEEP) DREAMING

List 1 dream you want to take a step towards this week and describe why it's important to you:

_____

_____

_____

STEP 2: TAKE ACTION

List at least 1 small but significant step you want to take towards this dream this week:

_____

_____

_____

STEP 3: SUSTAIN YOUR DREAMS

What's 1 small but significant thing you want to do to sustain your dream this week? (e.g. meet w/ someone, stop doing something, give someone a boost)

_____

_____

_____

Help others achieve their dreams and you will achieve yours.

LES BROWN

WEEK 21: _____ [DATE]

STEP 1: START (KEEP) DREAMING

List 1 dream you want to take a step towards this week and describe why it's important to you:

_____

_____

_____

STEP 2: TAKE ACTION

List at least 1 small but significant step you want to take towards this dream this week:

_____

_____

_____

STEP 3: SUSTAIN YOUR DREAMS

What's 1 small but significant thing you want to do to sustain your dream this week? (e.g. meet w/ someone, stop doing something, give someone a boost)

_____

_____

_____

> *Dream no small dreams for they have no*
> *power to move the hearts of men.*
> JOHANN WOLFGANG VON GOETHE

WEEK 22: _____ [DATE]

STEP 1: START (KEEP) DREAMING

List 1 dream you want to take a step towards this week and describe why it's important to you:

_____

_____

_____

STEP 2: TAKE ACTION

List at least 1 small but significant step you want to take towards this dream this week:

_____

_____

_____

STEP 3: SUSTAIN YOUR DREAMS

What's 1 small but significant thing you want to do to sustain your dream this week? (e.g. meet w/ someone, stop doing something, give someone a boost)

_____

_____

_____

> *It takes a lot of courage to show your dreams to someone else.*
>
> ERMA BOMBECK

WEEK 23: _____ [DATE]

STEP 1: START (KEEP) DREAMING

List 1 dream you want to take a step towards this week and describe why it's important to you:

_____

_____

_____

STEP 2: TAKE ACTION

List at least 1 small but significant step you want to take towards this dream this week:

_____

_____

_____

STEP 3: SUSTAIN YOUR DREAMS

What's 1 small but significant thing you want to do to sustain your dream this week? (e.g. meet w/ someone, stop doing something, give someone a boost)

_____

_____

_____

> *There are only two ways to live your life. One is as though nothing is a miracle. The other is as though everything is a miracle.*
>
> ALBERT EINSTEIN

WEEK 24: _____ [DATE]

STEP 1: START (KEEP) DREAMING

List 1 dream you want to take a step towards this week and describe why it's important to you:

_____

_____

_____

STEP 2: TAKE ACTION

List at least 1 small but significant step you want to take towards this dream this week:

_____

_____

_____

STEP 3: SUSTAIN YOUR DREAMS

What's 1 small but significant thing you want to do to sustain your dream this week? (e.g. meet w/ someone, stop doing something, give someone a boost)

_____

_____

_____

> ## *When you cease to dream you cease to live.*
> MALCOLM FORBES

WEEK 25: _____ [DATE]

STEP 1: START (KEEP) DREAMING

List 1 dream you want to take a step towards this week and describe why it's important to you:

_____

_____

_____

STEP 2: TAKE ACTION

List at least 1 small but significant step you want to take towards this dream this week:

_____

_____

_____

STEP 3: SUSTAIN YOUR DREAMS

What's 1 small but significant thing you want to do to sustain your dream this week? (e.g. meet w/ someone, stop doing something, give someone a boost)

_____

_____

_____

> *Life is inherently risky. There is only one big risk you should avoid at all costs, and that is the risk of doing nothing.*
>
> DENIS WAITLEY

WEEK 26: _____ [DATE]

STEP 1: START (KEEP) DREAMING

List 1 dream you want to take a step towards this week and describe why it's important to you:

_____

_____

_____

STEP 2: TAKE ACTION

List at least 1 small but significant step you want to take towards this dream this week:

_____

_____

_____

STEP 3: SUSTAIN YOUR DREAMS

What's 1 small but significant thing you want to do to sustain your dream this week? (e.g. meet w/ someone, stop doing something, give someone a boost)

_____

_____

_____

> *Create a definite plan for carrying out your desire and begin at once, whether you ready or not, to put this plan into action.*
>
> NAPOLEON HILL

WEEK 27: _____ [DATE]

STEP 1: START (KEEP) DREAMING

List 1 dream you want to take a step towards this week and describe why it's important to you:

_____

_____

_____

STEP 2: TAKE ACTION

List at least 1 small but significant step you want to take towards this dream this week:

_____

_____

_____

STEP 3: SUSTAIN YOUR DREAMS

What's 1 small but significant thing you want to do to sustain your dream this week? (e.g. meet w/ someone, stop doing something, give someone a boost)

_____

_____

_____

Do what you can, with what you have, where you are.
THEODORE ROOSEVELT

WEEK 28: _____ [DATE]

STEP 1: START (KEEP) DREAMING

List 1 dream you want to take a step towards this week and describe why it's important to you:

_____

_____

_____

STEP 2: TAKE ACTION

List at least 1 small but significant step you want to take towards this dream this week:

_____

_____

_____

STEP 3: SUSTAIN YOUR DREAMS

What's 1 small but significant thing you want to do to sustain your dream this week? (e.g. meet w/ someone, stop doing something, give someone a boost)

_____

_____

_____

> *Dreams are necessary to life.*
>
> ANAIS NIN

WEEK 29: _____ [DATE]

STEP 1: START (KEEP) DREAMING

List 1 dream you want to take a step towards this week and describe why it's important to you:

_____

_____

_____

STEP 2: TAKE ACTION

List at least 1 small but significant step you want to take towards this dream this week:

_____

_____

_____

STEP 3: SUSTAIN YOUR DREAMS

What's 1 small but significant thing you want to do to sustain your dream this week? (e.g. meet w/ someone, stop doing something, give someone a boost)

_____

_____

_____

Thinking will not overcome fear but action will.

W. CLEMENT STONE

WEEK 30: _____ [DATE]

STEP 1: START (KEEP) DREAMING

List 1 dream you want to take a step towards this week and describe why it's important to you:

_____

_____

_____

STEP 2: TAKE ACTION

List at least 1 small but significant step you want to take towards this dream this week:

_____

_____

_____

STEP 3: SUSTAIN YOUR DREAMS

What's 1 small but significant thing you want to do to sustain your dream this week? (e.g. meet w/ someone, stop doing something, give someone a boost)

_____

_____

_____

I believe that imagination is stronger than knowledge. That myth is more potent than history. That dreams are more powerful than facts. That hope always triumphs over experience. That laughter is the only cure for grief. And I believe that love is stronger than death.

ROBERT FULGHUM

WEEK 31: _____ [DATE]

STEP 1: START (KEEP) DREAMING

List 1 dream you want to take a step towards this week and describe why it's important to you:

_____

_____

_____

STEP 2: TAKE ACTION

List at least 1 small but significant step you want to take towards this dream this week:

_____

_____

_____

STEP 3: SUSTAIN YOUR DREAMS

What's 1 small but significant thing you want to do to sustain your dream this week? (e.g. meet w/ someone, stop doing something, give someone a boost)

_____

_____

_____

IGNITE

> *Never give up on what you really want to do. The person with big dreams is more powerful than the one with all the facts.*
>
> H. JACKSON BROWN, JR.

WEEK 32: _____ [DATE]

STEP 1: START (KEEP) DREAMING

List 1 dream you want to take a step towards this week and describe why it's important to you:

_____

_____

_____

STEP 2: TAKE ACTION

List at least 1 small but significant step you want to take towards this dream this week:

_____

_____

_____

STEP 3: SUSTAIN YOUR DREAMS

What's 1 small but significant thing you want to do to sustain your dream this week? (e.g. meet w/ someone, stop doing something, give someone a boost)

_____

_____

_____

An ant on the move does more than a dozing ox.

LAO TZU

WEEK 33: _____ [DATE]

STEP 1: START (KEEP) DREAMING

List 1 dream you want to take a step towards this week and describe why it's important to you:

_____

_____

_____

STEP 2: TAKE ACTION

List at least 1 small but significant step you want to take towards this dream this week:

_____

_____

_____

STEP 3: SUSTAIN YOUR DREAMS

What's 1 small but significant thing you want to do to sustain your dream this week? (e.g. meet w/ someone, stop doing something, give someone a boost)

_____

_____

_____

The path to success is to take massive, determined action.

TONY ROBBINS

WEEK 34: _____ [DATE]

STEP 1: START (KEEP) DREAMING

List 1 dream you want to take a step towards this week and describe why it's important to you:

_____

_____

_____

STEP 2: TAKE ACTION

List at least 1 small but significant step you want to take towards this dream this week:

_____

_____

_____

STEP 3: SUSTAIN YOUR DREAMS

What's 1 small but significant thing you want to do to sustain your dream this week? (e.g. meet w/ someone, stop doing something, give someone a boost)

_____

_____

_____

> *It is better to risk starving to death then surrender.*
> *If you give up on your dreams, what's left?*
>
> JIM CARREY

WEEK 35: _____ [DATE]

STEP 1: START (KEEP) DREAMING

List 1 dream you want to take a step towards this week and describe why it's important to you:

_____

_____

_____

STEP 2: TAKE ACTION

List at least 1 small but significant step you want to take towards this dream this week:

_____

_____

_____

STEP 3: SUSTAIN YOUR DREAMS

What's 1 small but significant thing you want to do to sustain your dream this week? (e.g. meet w/ someone, stop doing something, give someone a boost)

_____

_____

_____

> *The more credit you give away, the more will come back to you.*
> *The more you help others, the more they will want to help you.*
>
> BRIAN TRACY

WEEK 36: _____ [DATE]

STEP 1: START (KEEP) DREAMING

List 1 dream you want to take a step towards this week and describe why it's important to you:

_____

_____

_____

STEP 2: TAKE ACTION

List at least 1 small but significant step you want to take towards this dream this week:

_____

_____

_____

STEP 3: SUSTAIN YOUR DREAMS

What's 1 small but significant thing you want to do to sustain your dream this week? (e.g. meet w/ someone, stop doing something, give someone a boost)

_____

_____

_____

> *There are too many people praying for the mountains of difficulty to be removed, when what they really need is the courage to climb them.*
>
> RAILI A. JEFFERY

WEEK 37: _____ [DATE]

STEP 1: START (KEEP) DREAMING

List 1 dream you want to take a step towards this week and describe why it's important to you:

_____

_____

_____

STEP 2: TAKE ACTION

List at least 1 small but significant step you want to take towards this dream this week:

_____

_____

_____

STEP 3: SUSTAIN YOUR DREAMS

What's 1 small but significant thing you want to do to sustain your dream this week? (e.g. meet w/ someone, stop doing something, give someone a boost)

_____

_____

_____

*And the day came when the risk to remain tight in a bud
was more painful than the risk it took to blossom.*

ANAIS NIN

WEEK 38: _____ [DATE]

STEP 1: START (KEEP) DREAMING

**List 1 dream you want to take a step towards this week and describe why it's
important to you:**

_____

_____

_____

STEP 2: TAKE ACTION

**List at least 1 small but significant step you want to take towards this dream
this week:**

_____

_____

_____

STEP 3: SUSTAIN YOUR DREAMS

**What's 1 small but significant thing you want to do to sustain your dream
this week?** (e.g. meet w/ someone, stop doing something, give someone a boost)

_____

_____

_____

> *What counts is not necessarily the size of the dog in the fight; it's the size of the fight in the dog.*
>
> DWIGHT EISENHOWER

WEEK 39: _____ [DATE]

STEP 1: START (KEEP) DREAMING

List 1 dream you want to take a step towards this week and describe why it's important to you:

_____

_____

_____

STEP 2: TAKE ACTION

List at least 1 small but significant step you want to take towards this dream this week:

_____

_____

_____

STEP 3: SUSTAIN YOUR DREAMS

What's 1 small but significant thing you want to do to sustain your dream this week? (e.g. meet w/ someone, stop doing something, give someone a boost)

_____

_____

_____

> *Repetition of the same thought or physical action develops into a habit which, repeated frequently enough, becomes an automatic reflex.*
>
> NORMAN VINCENT PEALE

WEEK 40: _____ [DATE]

STEP 1: START (KEEP) DREAMING

List 1 dream you want to take a step towards this week and describe why it's important to you:

_____

_____

_____

STEP 2: TAKE ACTION

List at least 1 small but significant step you want to take towards this dream this week:

_____

_____

_____

STEP 3: SUSTAIN YOUR DREAMS

What's 1 small but significant thing you want to do to sustain your dream this week? (e.g. meet w/ someone, stop doing something, give someone a boost)

_____

_____

_____

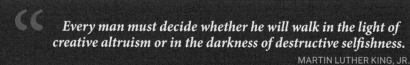

> *Every man must decide whether he will walk in the light of creative altruism or in the darkness of destructive selfishness.*
>
> MARTIN LUTHER KING, JR.

WEEK 41: _____ [DATE]

STEP 1: START (KEEP) DREAMING

List 1 dream you want to take a step towards this week and describe why it's important to you:

_____

_____

_____

STEP 2: TAKE ACTION

List at least 1 small but significant step you want to take towards this dream this week:

_____

_____

_____

STEP 3: SUSTAIN YOUR DREAMS

What's 1 small but significant thing you want to do to sustain your dream this week? (e.g. meet w/ someone, stop doing something, give someone a boost)

_____

_____

_____

> *I like the dreams of the future better
> than the history of the past.*
>
> THOMAS JEFFERSON

WEEK 42: _____ [DATE]

STEP 1: START (KEEP) DREAMING

List 1 dream you want to take a step towards this week and describe why it's important to you:

_____

_____

_____

STEP 2: TAKE ACTION

List at least 1 small but significant step you want to take towards this dream this week:

_____

_____

_____

STEP 3: SUSTAIN YOUR DREAMS

What's 1 small but significant thing you want to do to sustain your dream this week? (e.g. meet w/ someone, stop doing something, give someone a boost)

_____

_____

_____

> *Be a first rate version of yourself, not a*
> *second rate version of someone else.*
>
> JUDY GARLAND

WEEK 43: _____ [DATE]

STEP 1: START (KEEP) DREAMING

List 1 dream you want to take a step towards this week and describe why it's important to you:

_____

_____

_____

STEP 2: TAKE ACTION

List at least 1 small but significant step you want to take towards this dream this week:

_____

_____

_____

STEP 3: SUSTAIN YOUR DREAMS

What's 1 small but significant thing you want to do to sustain your dream this week? (e.g. meet w/ someone, stop doing something, give someone a boost)

_____

_____

_____

Never mistake motion for action.

ERNEST HEMINGWAY

WEEK 44: _____ [DATE]

STEP 1: START (KEEP) DREAMING

List 1 dream you want to take a step towards this week and describe why it's important to you:

_____

_____

_____

STEP 2: TAKE ACTION

List at least 1 small but significant step you want to take towards this dream this week:

_____

_____

_____

STEP 3: SUSTAIN YOUR DREAMS

What's 1 small but significant thing you want to do to sustain your dream this week? (e.g. meet w/ someone, stop doing something, give someone a boost)

_____

_____

_____

*The biggest adventure you can take is
to live the life of your dreams.*

OPRAH WINFREY

WEEK 45: _____ [DATE]

STEP 1: START (KEEP) DREAMING

List 1 dream you want to take a step towards this week and describe why it's important to you:

_____

_____

_____

STEP 2: TAKE ACTION

List at least 1 small but significant step you want to take towards this dream this week:

_____

_____

_____

STEP 3: SUSTAIN YOUR DREAMS

What's 1 small but significant thing you want to do to sustain your dream this week? (e.g. meet w/ someone, stop doing something, give someone a boost)

_____

_____

_____

> *The superior man acts before he speaks, and*
> *afterwards speaks according to his action.*
>
> CONFUCIUS

WEEK 46: _____ [DATE]

STEP 1: START (KEEP) DREAMING

List 1 dream you want to take a step towards this week and describe why it's important to you:

_____

_____

_____

STEP 2: TAKE ACTION

List at least 1 small but significant step you want to take towards this dream this week:

_____

_____

_____

STEP 3: SUSTAIN YOUR DREAMS

What's 1 small but significant thing you want to do to sustain your dream this week? (e.g. meet w/ someone, stop doing something, give someone a boost)

_____

_____

_____

I never worry about action, but only inaction.

WINSTON CHURCHILL

WEEK 47: _____ [DATE]

STEP 1: START (KEEP) DREAMING

List 1 dream you want to take a step towards this week and describe why it's important to you:

_____

_____

_____

STEP 2: TAKE ACTION

List at least 1 small but significant step you want to take towards this dream this week:

_____

_____

_____

STEP 3: SUSTAIN YOUR DREAMS

What's 1 small but significant thing you want to do to sustain your dream this week? (e.g. meet w/ someone, stop doing something, give someone a boost)

_____

_____

_____

> *Daring to set boundaries is about having the courage to love ourselves, even when we risk disappointing others.*
>
> BRENE BROWN

WEEK 48: _____ [DATE]

STEP 1: START (KEEP) DREAMING

List 1 dream you want to take a step towards this week and describe why it's important to you:

_____

_____

_____

STEP 2: TAKE ACTION

List at least 1 small but significant step you want to take towards this dream this week:

_____

_____

_____

STEP 3: SUSTAIN YOUR DREAMS

What's 1 small but significant thing you want to do to sustain your dream this week? (e.g. meet w/ someone, stop doing something, give someone a boost)

_____

_____

_____

Prayer is where the action is.

JOHN WESLEY

WEEK 49: _____ [DATE]

STEP 1: START (KEEP) DREAMING

List 1 dream you want to take a step towards this week and describe why it's important to you:

_____

_____

_____

STEP 2: TAKE ACTION

List at least 1 small but significant step you want to take towards this dream this week:

_____

_____

_____

STEP 3: SUSTAIN YOUR DREAMS

What's 1 small but significant thing you want to do to sustain your dream this week? (e.g. meet w/ someone, stop doing something, give someone a boost)

_____

_____

_____

> *The chief condition on which, life, health and vigor depend on, is action. It is by action that an organism develops its faculties, increases its energy, and attains the fulfillment of its destiny.*
>
> COLIN POWELL

WEEK 50: _____ [DATE]

STEP 1: START (KEEP) DREAMING

List 1 dream you want to take a step towards this week and describe why it's important to you:

_____

_____

_____

STEP 2: TAKE ACTION

List at least 1 small but significant step you want to take towards this dream this week:

_____

_____

_____

STEP 3: SUSTAIN YOUR DREAMS

What's 1 small but significant thing you want to do to sustain your dream this week? (e.g. meet w/ someone, stop doing something, give someone a boost)

_____

_____

_____

> *There's always ways of motivating yourself to higher levels. Write about it, dream about it. But after that, turn it into action. Don't just dream.*
>
> DAN GABLE

WEEK 51: _____ [DATE]

STEP 1: START (KEEP) DREAMING

List 1 dream you want to take a step towards this week and describe why it's important to you:

_____

_____

_____

STEP 2: TAKE ACTION

List at least 1 small but significant step you want to take towards this dream this week:

_____

_____

_____

STEP 3: SUSTAIN YOUR DREAMS

What's 1 small but significant thing you want to do to sustain your dream this week? (e.g. meet w/ someone, stop doing something, give someone a boost)

_____

_____

_____

> *Half of the troubles of this life can be traced to saying yes too quickly and not saying no soon enough.*
>
> JOSH BILLINGS

WEEK 52: _____ [DATE]

STEP 1: START (KEEP) DREAMING

List 1 dream you want to take a step towards this week and describe why it's important to you:

_____

_____

_____

STEP 2: TAKE ACTION

List at least 1 small but significant step you want to take towards this dream this week:

_____

_____

_____

STEP 3: SUSTAIN YOUR DREAMS

What's 1 small but significant thing you want to do to sustain your dream this week? (e.g. meet w/ someone, stop doing something, give someone a boost)

_____

_____

_____

Meet the IGNITE Team

AUTHOR MITCH MATTHEWS

Mitch Matthews is a leading authority on innovative thinking, human performance and goal achievement.

But he's probably best known simply as… "The big dream guy."

This is due in part to his passion for inspiring people to think about their big dreams and put a plan in place to achieve them. And… partly because of his own big dream of helping to launch one million big dreams in his lifetime.

He has worked with leaders and teams from organizations like NASA, Disney, Dupont Pioneer, Booking.com and the Principal Financial Group.

In 2006, Mitch and his wife started something called the BIG Dream Gathering. These events have helped thousands of people to dream bigger and, in many cases, get the boost they needed to get their big dreams accomplished.

Mitch also works one-on-one with people as an Elite Executive Coach. Plus, he has created a life coach training program that has been utilized around the globe.

His biggest dream and his greatest adventure involves being a husband to his incredible wife Melissa and a dad to their two amazing sons.

If you would like to connect with Mitch or have him come to speak to your organization, you can find him at **MitchMatthews.com**.

And a special thank you to Marty and Cheri Doane, and to amazing people like them, who see a dream in a 13-year-old kid and ignite it!

VISUAL AUTHOR JOCELYN WALLACE

Jocelyn has had her fair share of igniting BIG dreams, both for herself and for others. After working for many years in the corporate business world, she founded Red Eleven Group, LLC.

As visual author of this book she partnered with the Matthews Group to create original, exclusive photography and a book experience with a simple aim: 1.) co-create ideas, 2.) visually translate stories & meaning and 3.) encourage, challenge and inspire readers.

If you are an author and you want to take your book to the next level, you need Jocelyn! She facilitates idea eruptions, coaches writing blocks, and contributes her passion for storytelling and teaching within her written work. When needed, Jocelyn helps create strategies to repurpose content into products, trainings, and keynote deliveries for various distribution channels.

But that's not all. Jocelyn is also a speaker and business/life coach. There's an interesting twist to her approach, whether she is speaking, teaching, or coaching business professionals. She makes all ideas VISUAL and teaches you how to do it too

Jocelyn has been honored to speak on visual learning at conferences and workshops around the world. With a focus on strategic visioning and creative leadership, she teaches teams how to change stagnant business cultures into idea-rich playgrounds. Simply put, she does cool stuff!

When Jocelyn isn't working or writing about visual thinking on her blog, she's all about spending time with loved ones. As wife of an amazing guy and mom of two, she knows the challenges of balancing career and family. They just hope she doesn't start any more fires with her cooking or back her car into any more buildings!

If you want to connect with Jocelyn or invite her to speak at your next event, catch her if you can at JocelynWallace.com.

ARTIST MELISSA JOHNSON-MATTHEWS

We are honored and blessed to feature some original art from Mitch's wife, Melissa Johnson-Matthews, on the cover and throughout the book. She's got a great story and an amazing heart. The world needs more of her gifts!

If you'd like to find out more about Melissa and her art, you can visit: MelissaJohnsonMatthews.com.

IGNITE PROJECT MANAGER LISE CARTWRIGHT

Lise has always looked for the magic in life - "I'm not talking about the 'make-an-elephant-disappear' or 'pull-a-rabbit-outta-the-hat' type of magic – although that's cool – I'm talking about the magic of relationships."

Lise is passionate about following her dreams, with her daily mantra "do what you love" ringing in her ears, she meets life head-on with a quick skip in her step and a big smile on her face. She is a self-published author and writer and enjoys helping others achieve their dreams.

If you'd like to find out more about Lise and what she does, you can visit: about.me/lisecartwright